WHO, WHAT, WHY?

WHY DID
THE EXODUS
HAPPEN?

DANIKA COOLEY

CF4

10 9 8 7 6 5 4 3 2 1
Copyright © Danika Cooley 2024
Paperback ISBN: 978-1-5271-1176-9
ebook ISBN: 978-1-5271-1241-4

Published by
Christian Focus Publications,
Geanies House, Fearn, Tain, Ross-shire,
IV20 1TW, Scotland, U.K.
www.christianfocus.com
email: info@christianfocus.com

Printed and bound by Bell and Bain, Glasgow

Cover design by Catriona Mackenzie
Illustrations by Martyn Smith

TABLE OF CONTENTS

Dedication

To the Reader (That's you!)
May you spend your life learning to know
our great God.

THE AUTHOR

Danika Cooley and her husband, Ed, are committed to leading their children to live for the glory of God. Danika has a passion for equipping parents to teach the Bible and Christian history to their kids. She is the author of *Help Your Kids Learn and Love the Bible; When Lightning Struck!: The Story of Martin Luther; Bible Investigators: Creation; Wonderfully Made: God's Story of Life from Conception to Birth*, and the *Who, What, Why?* Series about the history of our faith. Danika's three year Bible survey curriculum, Bible Road Trip™, is used by families around the world. Weekly, she encourages tens of thousands of parents to intentionally raise biblically literate children. Danika is a homeschool mother of four with a Bachelor of Arts degree from the University of Washington. Find her at ThinkingKidsBlog.org.

GOD IS
FAITHFUL

Promises are hard to keep. After all, we don't know what will happen in life. Our plans might change because of a record-breaking blizzard, or an important family event. Sometimes, a person makes a convincing promise, then doesn't keep their side of the bargain. Maybe they forget—or maybe they just change their mind. Sometimes, even with the best of intentions, we break our promises.

There is one being in the whole universe, though, who never ever breaks his promises. Our great God, the King of the Universe, is faithful. What does that mean? God is steadfast—he never changes. God is the same yesterday, today, and tomorrow. We can trust God and depend on him and on his Word, the Bible. God never, ever breaks his promises and he always does what he says he will do! God is never surprised by events. In fact, God arranges everything that occurs. God is faithful—he never forgets his promises and he never changes.

A long time ago, God called a man named Abraham to follow him, to leave his home in the land of Ur, and to move to a new land. God made a number of promises to Abraham in Genesis chapter 15:

- Abraham's *offspring*—his children and his children's children (and so on!)—would be more numerous than the stars.

- His offspring would be *sojourners*—visitors staying in a land that was not theirs.

- In that land, Abraham's heirs would be *afflicted*—they would live in pain and distress—for four hundred years.

- Then, God would judge that nation for sinning against Abraham's offspring.

- God would bring Abraham's people out of the land, where they were oppressed, with great riches.

- Later, God would give his people the land of Canaan, also called the Promised Land.

God kept every one of the promises that he made to Abraham.

What happened after God's promise to Abraham, you ask? Well, Abraham served God. He and his wife,

Sarah, had a son, Isaac. Then, Isaac had two boys, Esau and Jacob. His offspring didn't outnumber the stars yet, but wait! Jacob had twelve sons, including Joseph. Then, Joseph's brothers sold him as a slave to the Midianites, a traveling people. The Midianites sold Joseph into slavery in Egypt.

Being a slave in Egypt must have been terrible, but Joseph had faith that God is faithful to keep his promises. Through an amazing series of events, God

made Joseph second-in-command in all of Egypt. Only Pharaoh, the king of Egypt, had more power than Joseph. There was a severe famine, but through Joseph's wisdom and God's guidance, Egypt had food. So, Joseph brought his family—all the men with their wives and children—to live in Goshen, Egypt, where the Nile River flows into the Mediterranean Sea. It was a beautiful place to live—temporarily.

The people of Israel—Jacob's children and their children, descended from Abraham and Isaac—lived

for hundreds of years in the land of Egypt. Eventually, Joseph's Pharaoh died, and another Pharaoh took his place. Then another and another until the Pharaoh in charge didn't remember Joseph.

The people of Israel became not just sojourners, but slaves. They lived in pain and distress for 430 years. Still, God blessed the people of Israel, and they grew and multiplied until there were more than two million men, women, and children enslaved in Egypt. There were so many Israelites that the wicked Pharaoh ordered that all Israelite baby boys should be killed.

In this time of suffering, a baby named Moses was saved by God. In fact, he was adopted by the Pharaoh's own daughter. Then, when Moses was forty, he saw an Egyptian beating an Israelite slave. Moses killed the Egyptian—an awful sin—and fled to live among the Midianites, the same desert people who once purchased Joseph as a slave.

The situation for the Israelites and for Moses sounds bleak, but God was already moving the events of history this way and that, keeping his promises to Abraham. God was faithful to Abraham, to Isaac, to Jacob, to Joseph, later to Moses, and then to the people of Israel, just as he is faithful now to all who believe in his Son, Jesus.

Our God wants us to know him. There is none like God in all the earth. He is holy, faithful, sovereign, our Savior, and all-powerful. God is always with us, always our caring provider, and always victorious. This is the story of the Exodus (the word means 'to depart from') and the people God led from Egypt. God used the Exodus event to teach his people who he is.

The story of the Exodus is about how a shepherd and his brother led a nation of slaves in opposition to the most powerful ruler of the world's most powerful kingdom. It's the story of one nation of people who served the Almighty Living God, and another nation whose citizens worshiped sticks, stones, frogs, and the sun. Most of all, this is the story of our amazing God and how he taught his people who he is.

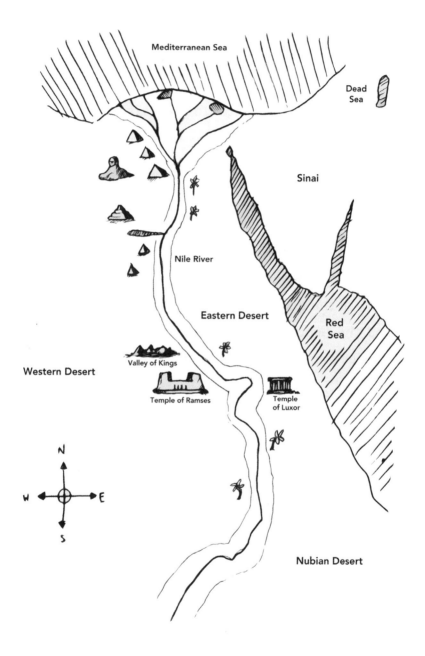

THE IDOLS OF EGYPT

God is our Creator, and King, the Ruler of all things. The Egyptians, though, worshiped creation rather than the Creator. They invented false gods—idols—that they believed ruled over nature like the River Nile and the animals of Egypt. Pharaohs of Egypt even pretended to be a sun god they called Amun-Ra.

During the Exodus, God repeatedly told Pharaoh through his prophet Moses to "let my people go." God performed many signs and wonders so everyone would know that he is the Lord—there is none like him in all the earth. No one in all of Egypt could make God's mighty signs stop—not Pharaoh or his magicians, and especially not the false idols of Egypt.

GOD IS
KNOWN TO US

In this world, there are a great many things to know. We can learn about algebra, art, biology, and even rocket science. But, no library of knowledge in this world is more important than knowing the one true God.

God told Pharaoh the Exodus happened "so that you may know there is none like me in all the earth."

God also said, over and over again, that the Exodus happened so "that you may know that I am the LORD" (Exodus 10:2b).

He even told Pharaoh, "But for this purpose I have raised you up, to show you my power, so that my name may be proclaimed in all the earth" (Exodus 9:16).

God wants us to know him.

After Moses fled from Egypt to live in the desert of Sinai as a shepherd, God blessed him with a wife—the daughter of a priest, Jethro—and two sons. Moses lived in the wilderness for forty years, in a sandy tent instead of a riverside palace.

One day, Moses was out near Mount Sinai, also called Mount Horeb, shepherding his sheep and goats. He noticed flames in a bush that was not burning up. From the bush, God called Moses by name, then told him to remove his sandals, for he was on holy ground.

At the burning bush, God made himself known to Moses. God said, "I am the God of your father, the God of Abraham, the God of Isaac, and the God of Jacob" (Exodus 3:6).

Then, God told Moses it was time for God to fulfill many of his promises to Abraham. God saw the pain of the Israelites while they were slaves to the Egyptians. So, God was going to rescue his people and lead them to the land he promised to Abraham.

God also promised to judge Egypt. Pharaoh would not let his people go unless God forced him. So, God would strike Egypt with many wonders. Only then would God bring the Israelites out of Egypt weighed down with great riches.

Moses asked God what name he should give the people of Israel as God's name. God replied, "I AM WHO I AM" (Exodus 3:14).

In Hebrew, "I AM" is translated YHWH. This can be pronounced *Yahweh*, which some translate into English as *Jehovah*. When you read LORD, with capital letters, that stands for the Hebrew name for God, Yahweh. "I AM" means that God IS. God always has been, he is, and he always will be. God was not created. Rather, he is the Creator of all things. God is the great

I AM, the Lord of heaven and earth, the commander of heaven's armies, the God who made himself known to Abraham, Moses, Israel—and to you.

God told Moses that he was going to send him to Pharaoh with a command to let God's people go. Moses was not thrilled about this. Not even a little bit. In fact, Moses gave God three great big excuses about why he could not take this message to Egypt's king.

First, Moses complained that the Israelites would not believe that God sent him. So, God gave him three signs to perform. In this way, God would make himself known to the Israelites. God told Moses to throw his staff on the ground where it became a snake. Moses tried it—and ran away. After Moses calmed down, he picked up the snake by its tail, and it was a staff again. Then, God told Moses to put his hand into his cloak where it became diseased with leprosy. Then, God healed it again. God gave Moses one last sign—water from the Nile River would turn to blood.

Still, Moses had more excuses. He told God he was a terrible speaker. God said he is the one who makes people speak the way they do, and he would teach Moses what to say. Moses objected one last time, asking God to send someone else. Now God was angry.

He told Moses he would send Moses' older brother, Aaron, to speak for him.

Moses was all out of excuses. Rather than make God angry again, he loaded his wife, Zipporah, and their two sons on a donkey and returned to the land of Pharaohs and pyramids, tombs and false gods. God promised Moses again that he would make himself known to Pharaoh. First, he would harden Pharaoh's heart so Pharaoh would not let God's people go. Then, God would do mighty works against Pharaoh.

God called Moses' brother, Aaron, to go into the wilderness to meet Moses. Together, they met with the people of Israel to make known God's special name, Yahweh. They told the Israelites God saw their pain and suffering, and he was going to keep his promise to Abraham. The people believed all that God said, and they worshiped him.

God has made himself known throughout time. He made himself known to the Israelites, then to the Egyptians, and now to us. In fact, God has given us a great big book about himself so that we can know the great I AM, our Creator. This book is the Bible. Isn't it wonderful that the King of heaven and earth wants you to know him? That's a perfect reason to worship him.

WHAT MOSES KNEW

When Pharaoh wickedly ordered Egyptians to kill all Israelite baby boys, Moses' mother set Moses in a waterproof basket in the Nile River. Pharaoh's daughter found and adopted the baby. Moses' older sister Miriam, who was hiding along the riverbank, volunteered to have her mother feed and care for Moses until he was a toddler.

By God's great plan, Moses spent his boyhood in the palace, surrounded by all the knowledge of the ancient Egyptians. He probably learned several languages and how to write legal documents. First, though, little Moses lived with his mother and father for three or four years. From his parents, Moses learned about the God of his people and the promises he made to his servant, Abraham.

GOD IS
SOVEREIGN

What happened next was not a battle between Moses and Pharaoh. Nor was it a battle between the Israelite God and the gods of the Pharaohs. It was not a battle at all, but a punishment from the Creator of the Universe in the form of ten plagues—diseases or judgments.

Remember, Pharaoh claimed to be a god. Egypt had many other false gods, too, like a frog goddess, cow goddesses, and even sky gods. None of these idols could stop the LORD from proving they were, in fact, fake.

When Moses and Aaron told Pharaoh that God said, "Let my people go," Pharaoh scoffed. "Who is this God? I don't know him." Then Pharaoh made life much, much harder for his slaves.

God reminded Moses he is the LORD—Yahweh. Our God is sovereign—the King of everything. He is in charge of time, nations, and rulers. God raised Pharaoh up to be king of an incredibly powerful nation. Then, God hardened Pharaoh's heart in order to show that God alone is the sovereign King.

Pharaoh's heart remained hard while Aaron's staff turned into a serpent. The staffs of Pharaoh's magicians also turned to serpents, but Aaron's serpent-staff ate them up!

BLOOD

Next, Moses hit the River Nile with his staff and it turned to blood. Aaron stretched out his staff and all the rivers, ponds, and even water in jugs turned to smelly blood. The fish died and everyone was thirsty. Pharaoh's magicians could also turn water into blood. But, they couldn't turn the Nile back into water. Pharaoh's heart was hard for a whole week while the waters of Egypt stood bloody.

FROGS

Next, Aaron held his staff over the waters and God sent frogs into Egypt and into Goshen—where the people of Israel lived. Frogs were everywhere: in jugs of water, in bread dough, even on the faces of sleeping people. Pharaoh's magicians could make frogs come out of the waters, but they couldn't make them go back in. Once Pharaoh promised to let God's people go, God caused the frogs to die. Piles of stinking, rotting frogs filled Egypt. Then, Pharaoh hardened his lying heart.

GNATS

God sent gnats all over Egypt and Goshen. Have you ever walked through a cloud of gnats? They get up your nose and in your eyes. This time, God didn't warn Pharaoh. Aaron hit the earth with his staff, and gnats were everywhere. The magicians couldn't make gnats, so they told Pharaoh, "This is the finger of God" (Exodus 8:19). Still, Pharaoh turned his hard heart against the sovereign King of the Universe.

FLIES

God sent Moses to say again, "Let my people go." Swarms of flies filled Egypt—but not Goshen. God spared the Israelites so Pharaoh would see God is sovereign over the earth. Now, Pharaoh tried to bargain with Moses. "Just sacrifice to God here in Egypt." But, Moses insisted God's people needed to sacrifice to the Lord after traveling three days into the wilderness. As the flies winged away, Pharaoh hardened his heart and would not let God's people go.

DEAD LIVESTOCK

Moses told Pharaoh to let God's people go before God sent a terrible plague on all of Egypt's livestock, but Pharaoh just shrugged his shoulders. His heart remained hard. Pharaoh still did not recognize that

God is, indeed, all powerful. His own false gods were not even real. And so, horses and donkeys, camels and sheep, goats and cows died in Egypt. In Goshen, the Israelites did not lose one lamb. Yet, Pharaoh's heart was hardened and he would not let God's people go.

BOILS

Next, Moses and Aaron threw handfuls of ashes into the air before Pharaoh. Ash blew all across Egypt. Wherever it landed, nasty boils full of pus covered the skin of people and animals. Pharaoh's magicians were so covered in boils they couldn't even appear in Pharaoh's court to talk to Moses. Still, God hardened Pharaoh's heart inside his boil-covered chest.

HAIL

Through Moses, God warned the Egyptians to bring their servants and livestock in from the fields. Pharaoh did nothing to protect his people or his animals, but some people in Egypt believed God. They hurried to protect their animals and servants. When hail, thunder and fire rained down on the fields, plants and trees were broken, unprotected cows were killed—even people died in the fields. Pharaoh admitted that he had sinned. He begged Moses and Aaron to pray to God. Yet when the fire and hail stopped, Pharaoh hardened his heart again.

LOCUSTS

God sent locusts, which are like giant grasshoppers that travel in swarms. The locusts ate anything not smashed by the hail—the trees and grain and vegetables. Again, Pharaoh confessed that he had sinned against God, and again he begged Moses to plead with God. So, God sent a great wind to blow away the locusts. Yet again, God hardened Pharaoh's heart.

DARKNESS

Egypt was pitch black for three days. No one could see anything. There were no stars, and there was no sun. Finally, Pharaoh told Moses to take his people and their little children and go. But, he said, you cannot bring your livestock. Once again, God hardened Pharaoh's heart.

THE GOD OF HEARTS

God is sovereign over everything, even hearts. The Bible tells us that God decided ahead of time that people who refuse to follow him will suffer his wrath. Some people will be punished in order to show the world that God is the Lord of All.

Now, Pharaoh hardened his own heart when he refused to follow God, even claiming to be a god. What a terrible sin! God kept Pharaoh's heart hard so that all the world would know that God is the Sovereign Lord.

The Bible carries a strong warning in Psalm 95:7b-8a: "Today, if you hear his voice, do not harden your hearts ..." We remind our hearts that God is King by praising him as our Lord!

GOD IS
OUR SAVIOR

Have you ever disobeyed your parents? Maybe you didn't clean your room like they asked. Our sovereign God placed your parents as authorities in your life, and he expects you to honor them. Disobeying your parent as a child is a sin. A sin is a thought or action that breaks God's law. Not cleaning your room when your mom asks may not seem like a big deal. Because you are breaking God's law, though, it is a big deal.

God's Word tells us that the punishment for sin—even just one sin—is death. In Jesus, though, there is life forever with God. Romans 6:23 says: "For the wages of sin is death, but the free gift of God is eternal life in Christ Jesus our Lord."

In Egypt, God's people were still in slavery to the wicked Pharaoh. Pharaoh's heart was hardened by sin, and he refused to believe in the Lord God, Yahweh. Even after Moses and Aaron told Pharaoh that God was going to kill all the firstborn sons in Egypt, Pharaoh did not repent—he did not turn from his sins and believe in God. Pharaoh's hard-heartedness was especially terrible since he had a firstborn son of his own. Pharaoh loved his sin so much that he kept sinning against God, even though it meant his son would die.

God prepared his people to leave Egypt. First, God fulfilled his promise to bring his people out of slavery with riches by having the Israelites ask their Egyptian neighbors for silver, gold, clothing, and jewelry. The people of Egypt gave the Israelites their treasures.

Next, God had each Israelite family bring a perfect lamb into their homes and live with it for five days. Then, as the sun was going down on the fifth day, each lamb was killed. Families painted the lamb's blood on the doorframe. This seems like a gruesome thing to do, doesn't it? It is.

The Lord was going to kill the firstborn sons in all the land of Egypt that very night. "On all the gods of Egypt I will execute judgments: I am the LORD," he declared (Exodus 12:12). God was making himself known—once

and for all—as the one, true God. The idols of Egypt had no power to stop the judgment of the Lord against the sin of the Egyptians who worshiped false gods.

But, God told his people that when the destroyer passed over a door painted in the blood of a perfect, flawless lamb, he would keep going. God would save the people in the house covered by the blood of the lamb. You see, the innocent lamb died to pay for the sins of the people in the house. Remember, the wages of sin is death. When the people heard that the Lord

provided a way of salvation for them, they worshiped God, their Savior. This event pointed toward the sacrifice Jesus, the true Lamb of God, later made for our eternal salvation.

As God instructed the Israelites through Moses, each family roasted their lamb, then ate it with unleavened bread and bitter herbs. It was very late by that time, but everyone in the family dined with their sandals on, their belts fastened, and their walking sticks in their hands. They were ready to go, because God was going to bring them out of Egypt!

At midnight, there was a terrible cry of grief from every single house in Egypt. The oldest son had died in the homes of Egyptian slaves. The captive in the palace dungeon lost his firstborn son, too. In the houses of the magicians and the royal servants, the oldest son died. Even the firstborn beasts died. Only the Israelites' homes were unharmed. Those homes where a lamb had died to take the punishment for sins.

When Pharaoh woke to the death of his oldest boy, he called Moses and Aaron to his home in the middle of the night. "Get out!" he cried. He told them to take all their people and their livestock and go serve the

Lord. The Egyptians were glad to see the people of Israel leave. They believed if the Israelites did not go, that all of Egypt would soon die.

The people of Israel left Egypt in the middle of the night with bowls of flatbread dough tied to their backs in their cloaks. They didn't even have time to bake it. There were six hundred thousand Israelite men walking out of Egypt. With their wives and children, the caravan probably numbered more than two million people.

Through the plagues, our sovereign God made himself known to the people of Egypt and to foreigners

living among the Egyptians. When the people of Israel left Egypt in the middle of the night, a great many people of different nationalities went with them. God is merciful—he saves anyone who repents of their sin and follows him.

God instructed the Israelites to eat the Passover feast every year as a way to remember the salvation of his people. The people would continue to eat the feast in the land God promised them. That way, their children would know that God had passed over their houses, which were covered in the blood of the lamb.

GOD'S GREAT PLAN FOR SALVATION

Once, in John 1:29b, John the Baptist saw Jesus and announced, "Behold, the Lamb of God, who takes away the sin of the world!" Jesus is the Son of God—a perfect, sinless man. He is also God the Son. Jesus died on a cross to take the punishment for the sin of all who believe in him and who repent of their sin.

While the Passover lamb died to spare people the judgment of death, the salvation offered was only temporary. Jesus Christ died so that those who believe in him and turn from their sin can live forever with God. The Lamb of God offers salvation from the slavery of sin for all eternity.

GOD IS
WITH US

The families of Israel left the land of Egypt with only their uncooked flatbread, livestock, walking sticks, and anything they could load into the packs on their animals. In spite of that, God brought this little nation of two million people out of the strongest country on earth with great riches. They had gold, silver, jewelry, and clothing from the Egyptians. They also carried with them flax to make linen and the leather of a Mediterranean sea animal—probably the dugong, which is a sea cow. Later, the Israelites would dedicate many of these materials to the Lord, using them to build a tabernacle where they could worship him.

Moses carried the bones of Joseph as he left Egypt. Before his death around four hundred years earlier, Joseph made his sons and nephews promise to carry his bones back to Canaan. Joseph trusted the promise our faithful God made to Abraham, so he knew that one day God's people would depart from Egypt, great in number and in possessions.

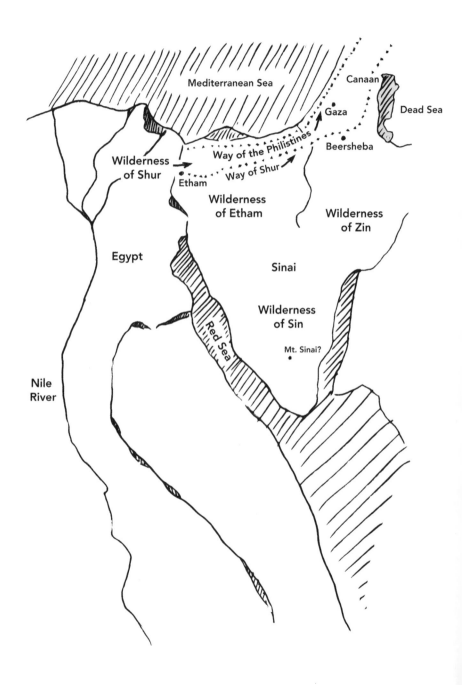

The Bible tells us that the people of Israel were ready for battle. Still, it must have been frightening for the Israelites to leave the only home they had ever known, setting out toward the wilderness in the middle of the night with no streetlamps to light the way. There were, however, roads.

Even in the days of ancient nations, around 3,500 years ago, people traveled from one place to another to trade animals, spices, and materials with other parts of the world. There was a road called the Way of the Philistines that provided a direct route between Egypt and the Land of Canaan. Now, God could have taken Moses and the Israelites straight to Canaan. However, that route ran right through the territory of the war-loving Philistines. Because that would frighten the people, God led them into the wilderness toward the Red Sea.

Have you ever hiked in nature while it is dark? Even with your family and friends around you, it can be quite frightening. God did not send the little children of Israel and their parents into the wilderness alone. Instead, he went with them. The people traveled out of Goshen to Succoth, then to Etham on the edge of the wilderness, where they set up camp.

During the day, God led the Israelites from a magnificent pillar of cloud. At night, he showed his glory by traveling before them in a bright pillar of fire. Imagine how large the pillar must have been to be visible to more than two million people. The pillar of cloud by day and the pillar of fire by night did not depart from the people. God was with his people, leading them, caring for them, and showing them some of his incredible beauty and majesty.

Like the pillar of cloud and fire, God is high and lifted up. He is not like us. He is not a created being who can be tired, hungry, or sad. Instead, God is our Creator. He made each one of us. No one created God. He has always been God.

Isn't it amazing that the Creator of the Universe desires to be with us, his created people? Even though God is high and lifted up like a pillar of fire, he is "actually not far from each one of us" (Acts 17:27). God was with Moses and the people of Israel all through the wilderness for forty years. He had the people build a tabernacle—a traveling temple—as a place to worship him.

Something you will want to know—that is a great mystery—is that God is three Persons in one. God is

one God. He is God the Father, God the Son (who is Jesus) and God the Holy Spirit. All three Persons of God are one God.

When God the Son, Jesus, was born of a virgin on earth, he became fully God and fully man. Jesus, therefore, lived a perfect, sinless life. While on earth, Jesus taught his people how to live for him. Then, like the perfect lamb at Passover, Jesus shed his blood as payment for their sins. He died in the place of each person who believes in him and repents of their sin, so

that one day every believer can live forever with God on the new earth.

Our faithful, sovereign God has made himself known to us. He is also with us, if we love him. While speaking to his prophet Jeremiah many years after the Exodus, God said in Jeremiah 9:23-24a, "Thus says the LORD: 'Let not the wise man boast in his wisdom, let not the mighty man boast in his might, let not the rich man boast in his riches, but let him who boasts boast in this, that he understands and knows me, that I am the LORD who practices steadfast love, justice, and righteousness in the earth.'" We should only boast in knowing God through his Son, Jesus.

GOD DWELLS IN HIS PEOPLE

Just as God has been with his people through the Exodus, as a pillar of fire and smoke, and then in the Most Holy Place in the Tabernacle, God is still with his people today. He dwells with them.

God's Word, the Bible, tells us that a little over 2,000 years ago, Jesus lived a perfect life and died for the sins of all who believe in him and repent of their sins. God gave us the Bible, his Word, so that we can know him. God also dwells in every Christian.

Before Jesus was crucified, resurrected, and then ascended to heaven, he taught us about the Holy Spirit living in God's people. In John 14:16-17, Jesus said: "And I will ask the Father, and he will give you another Helper, to be with you forever, even the Spirit of truth, whom the world cannot receive, because it neither sees him nor knows him. You know him, for he dwells with you and will be in you."

GOD IS
ALL-POWERFUL

From their camp at Etham on the edge of the wilderness, God directed Moses to turn back and lead the people to camp between Migdol and the Red Sea. Why would God do that? After all, the people were fleeing slavery to the Egyptians—they probably wanted to get as far away as possible.

God had a bigger plan. God said to Moses: "And I will harden Pharaoh's heart, and he will pursue them, and I will get glory over Pharaoh and all his host, and the Egyptians shall know that I am the LORD" (Exodus 14:4). The king of Egypt had claimed to be a god, defying the one, true God and harming his people. In one final judgment, God was going to show that only he deserved the honor and glory Pharoah tried to take for himself.

Pharaoh and many in his army lost their sons. They should have been at home mourning. But, when Pharaoh heard that the Israelites had left Egypt, he and his servants were filled with rage.

Imagine standing in the camp of Israel, alongside the sea. As you look toward Egypt, you spot a massive cloud of sand rising toward the sky. Over time, you feel the rumble of the earth and see 600 of Egypt's fastest chariots, drawn by its fastest horses, with its most vicious warriors racing toward you. Behind that, the rest of Egypt's army is headed your way. It would be terrifying knowing you had to face the most powerful army on earth.

The terrified Israelites cried out to God for help. Now, praying to our faithful, sovereign, powerful Savior God is always the right thing to do. We can trust our good God, knowing everything is under God's powerful control. But, the Israelites also gave in to their fear. They asked Moses why he brought them to die in the wilderness. "Didn't we tell you to leave us alone in Egypt?" they wailed.

Moses knew our powerful God. He said, "Fear not, stand firm, and see the salvation of the LORD, which he will work for you today. For the Egyptians whom you see today, you shall never see again. The LORD will fight for you, and you have only to be silent" (Exodus 14:13-14). God, of course, had a marvelous plan.

God told Moses to stretch his staff over the Red Sea. Then, God's pillar of cloud and fire moved between the Israelites and the approaching army of Egypt. The Egyptians could not see through the cloud, but the people of God had fire to light up the night. God sent a strong east wind that blew all night, parting the waters to create a highway through the sea, with a wall of water on the left and a wall of water on the right. Then, all of God's people walked through the Red Sea.

God allowed the Egyptians to chase the Israelites right onto that sandy road through the waters. Once the people of Israel were on the other side, though, the Egyptians panicked as God slowed their chariot wheels. You see, the Egyptians suddenly realized that Yahweh is the one true God. "Let us flee from before Israel, for the LORD fights for them against the Egyptians," (Exodus 14:25) they cried. Moses stretched his hand over the sea as God instructed,

and the walls of water fell into their normal place. The wicked army of Pharaoh drowned, and the people of God were saved from their captors.

Sometimes we question the acts of God, wondering if he is truly merciful. Mercy is God's goodness toward us. In fact, God is both patient and merciful. He allows us time to repent and turn away from our sin toward him. The hard truth is that God does judge those who do not repent. That judgment is also an act of mercy. When God judged the wicked Pharaoh and his vengeful army, he saved the Israelites and the people traveling with them from certain destruction. Also, when God drowned Egypt's army, he made himself known—to the Israelites, the Egyptians, and to the surrounding people groups—the Philistines, the Edomites, the Moabites, and all the Canaanites.

Scripture tells us that the Israelites:

- saw God's great power

- feared the Lord—honored God and recognized his power and sovereignty

- believed in the Lord

- understood that God sent Moses as his messenger

There will be a final, eternal judgment for all unbelievers. However, judgment here on earth—like the plagues or the Red Sea—can be a great mercy, as God reminds us of his great power and his holiness. Disasters can give people time to recognize their need for a Savior, and through judgment on some, God sometimes brings eternal life to many.

The people of Israel recognized God's goodness and great power as they watched their enemies perish. Moses led them in a song praising the God who was with them, who made himself known to them. Then, Moses' sister Miriam led the women in dancing before God with tambourines. Joyfully, they sang:

"I will sing to the LORD,

for he has triumphed gloriously;

the horse and rider he has thrown into the sea"

(Exodus 15:1).

ALL WILL KNOW HE IS THE LORD

When God created the heavens and the earth, he also ordered the world. Scripture tells us all things were created by Jesus, and he holds all things together. Sometimes, God overrules his natural order, creating a situation that could never exist without his intervention. The Egyptians called this "the finger of God" (Exodus 8:19).

God said he would do miracles through Moses in Egypt, then God used miracles to fulfill his promise that his name would be proclaimed in all the earth. While some miracles are wonderful, like a healing, and some are terrible, like water turning to blood, miracles are always extraordinary works of our all-powerful God that wouldn't occur normally.

GOD IS
OUR PROVIDER

After the people of God crossed the Red Sea, they followed Moses in the wilderness for three long, thirsty days. At Marah—which means bitterness—the water was terribly bitter, and they were unable to drink it. The Israelites grumbled against Moses, as they often did when things went poorly. As usual, Moses asked God for help. The Lord had Moses throw a log into the water, and the water suddenly became sweet. This was a miracle, because logs do not naturally cure terrible water.

Moses told the people to diligently listen to the voice of the Lord, their God. They must do what is right in God's eyes and obey his commands. If they were careful to follow God, he would not bring on them the diseases he brought upon the Egyptians. God told the people, "For I am the LORD, your healer" (Exodus 15:26). God cares for his people.

It must have been such a relief to have so much good water available when the people camped at Elim, an oasis with twelve springs and seventy palm trees.

From Elim, God led his people into the wilderness of Sin. The people grumbled and grumbled, then they grumbled some more. They wished they were back in Egypt where there was meat and bread, and they thought they might starve in the wilderness. Moses reminded the Israelites that they were really complaining about how God cared for them.

God waited until the people asked for food—though they did not ask nicely—before he promised to send bread from heaven six mornings each week. With God's people gathered before his glory shining in the pillar of cloud, God told Moses he heard the people's

grumbling. God would give them meat at twilight. "Then," God said, "you shall know that I am the LORD your God." That evening, a giant flock of quail—cute little birds you can hold in your hand—flew into the camp. What a feast!

The next morning, thin, sweet flakes of white bread from heaven covered the ground. When the people walked out of their tents and saw flakes on the ground like snow, they said, "Man hu?", which in Hebrew means "What is it?" *Man hu* sounds like manna, so that's what everyone called it. Instead of thanking God for food, they wrinkled their noses and asked

what they were looking at. Even the word they used for their daily bread sounded like grumbling.

When the sun heated the earth in the late morning, the manna melted. Some people stored manna for the next day, but found it was stinky and full of worms. However, on Friday mornings, when every family gathered double their usual amount for the Sabbath—a day of rest—there would be no worms in the manna the following day. It was a way God cared for them.

At Rephidim, the people camped and found no water to drink once again. Perhaps you expect the people finally prayed to God, asking him to meet their needs. After all, God was their caring provider who had given them sweet water, flocks of quail, and bread from heaven. But, no. Instead, the people grumbled their way right over to Moses and demanded water.

Moses reminded them they were grumbling against God. In fact, the people were testing the Lord— demanding that God prove he is faithful. Even so, the Israelites whined. Moses prayed to God, asking him what to do with the grumbling grumblers.

God had Moses walk before the people with some of the leaders of Israel. Moses obeyed God and struck a rock at Horeb in front of the elders. Clear water came pouring out. Moses named the place Massah and Meribah, which means testing and quarreling.

Living in the wilderness, camping in tents, and eating manna and quail was difficult. Yet, God caringly provided for his people. Rather than grumble, they were to bring their needs to him. Instead, they grumbled and whined and complained. Our caring God is very patient when we sin.

Many years before the Exodus, God promised Abraham that his offspring would be numerous and that they would be afflicted in a land that was not theirs for four hundred years. Then, God said, he would judge the nation that enslaved his people. He promised to bring them out of that land with great riches, and to lead them to the land of Canaan, which he promised to give them.

Our God is faithful, powerful, and sovereign. He is known to us, he is with us, and he cares for us. God kept his promises to the people of Israel, leading them out of Egypt while judging their captors. Because the people grumbled and tested God, refusing to trust him, God kept them in the desert for forty years before leading their children to the Promised Land.

Abraham, indeed, has many offspring. After Jesus lived on earth and died for the sins of all who believe in him, and after he rose from the dead, the apostle Paul wrote to the church. In Galatians 3:29, he said, "And if you are Christ's, then you are Abraham's offspring, heirs according to promise." Are you a believer in Jesus? Have you turned from your sin? Then you, too, are Abraham's offspring!

GOD WORKS IN OUR LIVES TODAY

It's easy to read the story of the Israelites and wonder why they were so busy grumbling, instead of thanking God for his blessings. You and I have never seen bread from heaven on the ground when we wake up. Still, we remember that our food comes from God—even when we buy it at the grocery store.

When Jesus taught his disciples how to pray, he told them to ask God for their food: "Give us each day our daily bread" (Luke 11:3). When we thank God before our meals, that's a way to remember that he provided for our daily needs. Everything we have comes from God. He is still our caring provider today.

GOD IS
VICTORIOUS

Do you remember what God declared about his work judging Egypt and rescuing the Israelites? He said, repeatedly, that the Exodus happened "that you may know that I am the Lord." God had a plan, all along, for his people to know him as their faithful, sovereign, all-powerful, caring, victorious Savior. Not only that, God's marvelous plan meant the Philistines, the people of Egypt, Moab, Midian, Canaan, and all the other

countries surrounding the Sinai wilderness would also know that the LORD, Yahweh, is the great I AM. They, too, could worship the King of the Universe.

Now, God could have taken the Israelites by the direct route, straight from Egypt into the Promised Land of Canaan in just a few days. He didn't do that. The Israelites had spent hundreds of years in slavery in a pagan nation. They had learned about hundreds of fake gods, and witnessed many false ways to worship. God knew they needed to learn more about who he is and how to worship him correctly. God's people needed to trust him. So, he led them toward Mount Sinai, where he would teach them how to love him and love each other.

Now, as the people were trudging through the wilderness, following God's glory in the pillar of cloud, some of them fell behind. Brutal fighters from a fiery people, who were descended from Jacob's brother, Esau, prowled the wilderness looking for travelers to rob and kill. When the vicious Amalekite warriors saw the people struggling to keep up with the rest of the Israelites, they attacked.

Growing up as a prince in Egypt, Moses may well have led the Egyptian army to war. At this point, though, leading the Israelites into battle at Rephidim in the wilderness, Moses was over eighty years old. So, he instructed his young follower, Joshua, to choose men to fight against the Amalekites the next day.

The following morning, while Joshua led his soldiers into battle, Moses, Aaron, and their friend Hur stood on a hill overlooking the battle. Moses held his staff stretched over the skirmish and the people of Israel began to win the battle. As the fighting raged on, Moses grew tired. Whenever he lowered his staff, the Amalekites began to win. To help Moses remain faithful in his position, Aaron and Hur lugged a large stone over to Moses and helped him sit on it. Then, they stood on either side of him, holding up his hands. By the time the sun set, Joshua and his troops were victorious.

God told Moses to write the story of the Lord's victory over the Amalekites in a book. Moses wrote the words of the Lord in the first five books of the Bible. His account of God's victory against the Amalekites is in Exodus chapter 17.

Moses built an altar to worship the Lord, and named the altar "The Lord is my Banner." An army heading out to war in ancient times would carry a banner stating who they were fighting for. The Israelites fought under the banner of our one true God, and God gave them the victory. Many years later, King David of Israel said, "For the battle is the LORD'S" (1 Samuel 17:47). Our God is sovereign and powerful over all things, and all victory comes from him alone. When we have troubles in this life, we can pray to God and know he will fight our battles for us when we follow Jesus and live for his glory.

Now, Moses' father-in-law, Jethro the Midianite priest of God, heard about God's victory on behalf of the Israelites. Perhaps, too, he heard about the quail, the bread from heaven, and the water flowing from a rock. Through his many victories and caring provision for his people, the Lord God was making himself known.

So, Jethro brought Moses' wife Zipporah and his two sons, Gershom and Eliezer, to visit Moses. After the burning bush, Zipporah and the boys headed toward Egypt with Moses. At some point Moses sent them home to stay with Jethro. Now, Moses and the Israelites were camped at Mount Sinai and the Exodus from Egypt was complete.

God told Pharaoh, "But for this purpose I have raised you up, to show you my power, so that my name may be proclaimed in all the earth" (Exodus 9:16). Moses proclaimed to Jethro all that God had done, and Jethro was overjoyed. He said, "Blessed be the LORD, who has delivered you out of the hand of the Egyptians and out of the hand of Pharaoh and has delivered the people from under the hand of the Egyptians. Now I know that the LORD is greater than all gods, because in this affair they dealt arrogantly with the people" (Exodus 18:10-11). Jethro sacrificed to God, worshiping him with Moses, Aaron, and all the elders of Israel.

Today we are still talking about God's victorious name and what he did during the Exodus.

WE CAN TRUST GOD

God made himself known to all people. He is faithful, sovereign, all-powerful, and victorious. For those who oppose God, this is a terrifying truth. Just like Pharaoh, anyone who sets themselves against Yahweh makes themselves the god of their own life, and will face God's judgment.

But, there is wonderful news for those who believe in Jesus and turn from their sins to follow God. For his people, God is a caring provider and the Savior. He is always with us. Romans 8:28 says, "And we know that for those who love God all things work together for good, for those who are called according to his purpose." No matter how hard things feel, God will work all things for our good.

GOD IS HOLY

Three months after the people of Israel left Egypt, God brought them to Mount Sinai, also called Mount Horeb, in the wilderness—the same place Moses was called by God in the burning bush. The Israelites remained there for about two years while God gave his law for the people to Moses.

The first time Moses climbed up the mountain to speak to God, God declared that the people would be his "treasured possession among all peoples"—if they obeyed his voice and kept his covenant. God promised to make them a holy nation (Exodus 19:5-6).

What does the word holy mean? When we say an object, a person, or even a nation is holy, it means that it is set apart for—or dedicated to—God. But what does it mean to say that God is holy? God is perfect, righteous, and he never, ever sins. Revelation 4:8 tells us that in God's throne room, there are four living creatures who never stop saying, "Holy, holy, holy, is the Lord God Almighty, who was and is and is to come!"

The Lord God told the people to purify themselves and wash their clothes. On the third day after Moses met with him, everyone stood at the foot of Mount Sinai while a thick cloud with smoke, fire, thunder, and lightning lowered onto the mountain. There was a deafening trumpet blast. It must have been terrifying! In fact, the people were told that if they touched the holy mountain—it was set aside for God, you see— they would die. But, Moses was allowed to walk right up the mountainside to talk to God.

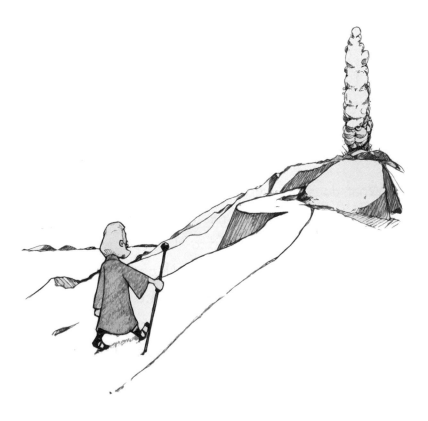

On Mount Sinai, God gave Moses three kinds of law for his people. First, he gave Moses the moral law. Because God is good, kind, loving, and faithful, we must also be good, kind, loving, and faithful to those around us. Because he is sovereign, all-powerful, victorious, and holy, we must fear—honor and respect—him as God alone. We love God and honor him as Lord, and we love our neighbors in the way the Ten Commandments tell us to. Do you know the Ten Commandments by heart? You can read God's Commandments in Exodus 20:1-17. Because the commands come from God's holy character, we still follow them today.

1. We are not to worship anyone or anything but God.

2. We must not make any images of God or of idols—false gods.

3. We must honor God's name—not abuse or misrepresent it.

4. We are to remember the Sabbath as holy. Today, Christians celebrate the Lord's Day on Sunday—the day when Jesus rose from the dead—by worshiping together and focusing on God.

5. We must honor our father and mother.

6. We must not murder.

7. We must not commit adultery—God made marriage to be a special promise before him.

8. We must not take anything that belongs to others.

9. We must not lie about another person to get them in trouble—that's called bearing false witness.

10. We must not desire to have—covet—anything which belongs to someone else.

These Commandments are ways God has given to us to show how we should love him and how to love others. God also gave two more types of law to his people. First, he gave them the civil law. Israel was a government run by God, without a king or a president.

God himself was the King of Israel, and he spoke to the people through his prophets—like Moses. The civil law taught Israel how to behave as a nation.

God also gave the people ceremonial law. That law taught people how to properly worship God. The ceremonial law also pointed to Jesus. God promised a Messiah who would save his people from their sins, and the way they worshiped him reminded them Jesus would come to save all who believed in him. The tabernacle, the feasts, and the system of sacrifices were all part of the ceremonial law.

At the beginning of his Ten Commandments, God said to Moses, "I am the LORD your God, who brought you out of the land of Egypt, out of the house of slavery" (Exodus 20:2). Long before God spoke to Moses on Mount Sinai, the Creator of heaven and earth made a promise to his servant, Abraham. At just the right time, God fulfilled his promise, bringing his people out of their oppression under the wicked rule of the Pharaoh of Egypt. While no one knows the real name of the Pharaoh of the Exodus—for Moses did not write it down—all people know the name of Yahweh, the Great I AM.

The Bible tells us the people of Israel left Egypt and took a "mixed multitude" with them. People from all nations chose to follow God rather than to stay in Egypt where false gods were worshiped. Today, people of all nations still set aside idols and false beliefs to follow our great God.

CAN ANYONE KEEP THE LAW?

Romans 3:10a says: "None is righteous, no, not one." You see, all have fallen short of God's glory—we all break his law and sin. Our sin separates us from God forever—and requires death as payment—which is terribly sad. The good news is that God allows us to live as his people, united with him through the death of a substitute—a pure, sinless, unblemished lamb.

The people of Israel had to sacrifice a lamb over and over again to cover their sins. So, God sent his Son, Jesus—who is God the Son and the Son of God—to be born fully God and fully human. Jesus lived a perfect, sinless life. Jesus, the Lamb of God, took the sins of all who believe in him on himself and he died to pay the punishment of our sin. Three days later, Jesus rose again, appeared to many people, then ascended to heaven.

God gave the apostle John a vision of eternity for all who love and follow Jesus. Revelation 21:3 says, "And I heard a loud voice from the throne saying, 'Behold, the dwelling place of God is with man. He will dwell with them, and they will be his people, and God himself will be with them as their God.'" One day, Jesus will return for his people, and we will live forever with God on the new earth—a mixed multitude of people from every nation, heirs of God's promise to Abraham!

TIMELINE

Note: The dating for the rule of Pharaohs in Ancient Egypt varies, as calendars varied. Also, there are two widely accepted dates for the Exodus. This timeline is based on the early date. The early date of the Exodus works backward from dates in Scripture, and is supported by many conservative scholars. Today, biblical scholars are still not entirely certain who the Pharaoh of the Exodus is.

c. 3000 BC

Upper and Lower Egypt unite, and Memphis is built on the boundary of the two to unite Egypt. The city was the capital of the Old Kingdom.

c. 2630 BC

The first pyramid, the Step Pyramid, is built in Saqqara, Egypt by Pharaoh Djoser. It takes twenty years to build.

c. 2560 BC

Pharaoh Khufu builds the Great Pyramid in Giza, Egypt. Originally 755 feet tall (now 481 feet), it is considered one of the Seven Wonders of the Ancient World—and the only one that still exists.

2166-1991 BC

The life of Abraham. God's covenant with Abraham establishes the Israelites as his chosen people.

2066 BC

Isaac, Abraham's son is born.

2006 BC

Jacob, Isaac's son, is born right after his twin brother, Esau. God later renames Jacob Israel. Jacob becomes the father of the twelve tribes of the nation of Israel.

c. 1971 BC

The Temple of Amun, the Egyptian false god of the sun, is built by Pharaoh Senusret I in Karnak, Egypt. The Karnak Temple Complex is used daily for over 1,700 years.

1915 BC

Joseph is born to Jacob and his wife, Rachel.

1886 BC

Isaac dies at 180 years old.

c. 1884 BC

Joseph becomes Egypt's second-in-command after being sold into slavery by his brothers.

c. 1876 BC

Perhaps the date that God brought Jacob's family to Goshen, Egypt, through Joseph.

1859 BC

Jacob dies in Goshen, after seventeen years in Egypt. He is 147 years old when he dies.

1805 BC

Joseph dies in Egypt at 110 years old. Joseph makes his brothers swear they will take his bones with them when God leads them out of Egypt.

c. 1750 BC

King Hammurabi rules Babylon and writes the Code of Hammurabi, 282 laws carved in stone. Moses would have studied this law code during his education in Egypt.

1570-1293 BC

The 18th Dynasty of Egypt is the strongest period of rule for Ancient Egypt.

1595 BC

The Hittites defeat Babylon.

c. 1570-1070 BC

The New Kingdom in Egypt. Thebes (now called Luxor) was the capitol of Egypt at the time. The temples of Luxor and Karnak were located in the city, with the Valley of the Kings burial ground just three miles outside the city.

1526 BC

Moses is born. His mother hides him in a basket in the Nile where the Pharaoh's daughter bathes. Pharaoh's daughter adopts Moses.

1504-1453 BC

Pharaoh Thutmose III reigns over Egypt. A tomb painting for his prime minister, Rehkmire, shows foreigners making bricks. Thutmose III expands his empire into Canaan.

1504-1483 BC

Hatshepsut rules as the only female Pharaoh. Some people think Hatshepsut may have been Moses' adoptive mother.

c. 1453-1425 BC

Pharaoh Amenhotep II reigns over Egypt. The early date for the Exodus would indicate that Amenhotep II was the Pharaoh of the Exodus. Scripture does not indicate that Pharaoh followed his army into the Red Sea.

1486 BC

Moses kills the Egyptian overseer at age forty. He flees Egypt and spends forty years as a shepherd in Midian.

c. 1450-1027 BC

The Shang Dynasty rules in China.

1446 BC

The Exodus happens, and Moses is eighty years old! The Israelites celebrate the first Passover and leave captivity in Egypt. This is the early date for the Exodus.

- The people bring the bones of Joseph out of Egypt with them.

- God gives instructions for the tabernacle and the Israelites construct the portable temple.

1446-1445 BC

The Israelites camp at Mount Sinai, where God gives them the Law. They make and worship the golden calf, sinning terribly.

1446-1406 BC

The Israelites remain in the wilderness.

1406 BC

Moses dies at 120 years of age. Joshua leads the Israelites as they begin their conquest of Canaan.

c. 1208 BC

Pharaoh Merneptah inscribes an account of his victory over ancient Libyans in stone. The Merneptah Stele mentions a battle against Israel in Canaan around 1230 BC. It is the oldest mention of Israel in writing that we have, outside of the Bible.

c. 1200 BC

The Hittite Empire collapses. The Hittites had controlled a huge territory, from Turkey, to parts of Syria and Lebanon.

c. 1164 BC

Egypt loses much of its power in the ancient world.

c. 966 BC

The Israelite Temple is finished and dedicated, built under Solomon, 480 years after the Exodus (1 Kings 6:1).

c. AD 30

Jesus is crucified. He is raised from the dead and ascends to heaven.

WORKS CONSULTED

Blaylock, Richard. "The Doctrine of Reprobation." The Gospel Coalition. https://www.thegospelcoalition.org/essay/doctrine-of-reprobation/. Accessed October 2022.

Boice, James Montgomery. *The Life of Moses: God's First Deliverer of Israel.* P&R Publishing, 2018.

Collins, John. "Miracles." The Gospel Coalition. https://www.thegospelcoalition.org/essay/miracles/. Accessed February 16, 2023.

Currid, John D. and David P. Barrett. *Crossway ESV Bible Atlas.* Crossway, 2010.

"Date of the Exodus." Evidence Unseen. https://www.evidenceunseen.com/date-of-the-Exodus/. Accessed October 2022.

Grudem, Wayne. *Systematic Theology: An Introduction to Biblical Doctrine.* Zondervan, 1995.

Hamilton, Adam. *Moses: In the Footsteps of the Reluctant Prophet.* Abingdon Press, 2017.

"How can I achieve victory in Jesus?" Got Questions Ministries. https://www.gotquestions.org/victory-in-Jesus.html. Accessed February 15, 2023.

Janzen, Mark D., Scott Stripling, James K. Hoffmeier, Peter Feinman, Gary A. Rendsburg, and Ronald Hendel. *Five Views on the Exodus: Historicity, Chronology, and Theological Implications.* Zondervan Academic, 2021.

Oliphant, Margaret. *The Atlas of the Ancient World: Charting the Great Civilizations of the Past.* Barnes & Noble Books, 1998.

Packer, J. I. *Knowing God.* InterVarsity Press, 2001.

Pink, Arthur. *The Attributes of God*. The New Christian Classics, 2018.

Rose Book of Bible Charts, Maps & Time Lines. Rose Publishing, 2010.

Rose Guide to the Tabernacle. Rose Publishing, 2016.

Sproul, R.C. "What is Providence?" Ligonier. https://www.ligonier.org/learn/articles/what-providence. Accessed February 15, 2023.

The ESV Study Bible™, ESV® Bible. Crossway, 2008.

Tozer, A.W. *The Attributes of God, Volume 1: A Journey into the Father's Heart*. WingSpread Publishers, 2007.

Tozer, A.W. *The Attributes of God, Volume 2: Deeper Into the Father's Heart*. WingSpread Publishers, 2007.

"What is divine providence?" Got Questions Ministries. https://www.gotquestions.org/divine-providence.html. Accessed February 15, 2023.

"What is the Shekinah glory?" Got Questions Ministries. https://www.gotquestions.org/shekinah-glory.html. Accessed February 15, 2023.

Christian Focus Publications publishes books for adults and children under its four main imprints: Christian Focus, CF4K, Mentor and Christian Heritage. Our books reflect our conviction that God's Word is reliable and Jesus is the way to know him, and live for ever with him.

Our children's publication list covers pre-school to early teens. We also publish personal and family devotional titles, biographies and inspirational stories that children will love.

From pre-school board books to teenage apologetics, we have it covered!

Christian Focus Publications Ltd,
Geanies House, Fearn, Ross-shire,
IV20 1TW, Scotland,
United Kingdom.
www.christianfocus.com